W9-DJF-795

Clara's Bakery

1865

BAKED
FRESH
DAILY

CLARA'S BAKERY

BUTCHER

COOKBOOK

Susan K. Jones
and
Carol Spielman Lezak

International Resourcing Services, Inc.
Northbrook, Illinois

Developed and produced by International Resourcing Services, Inc.,
and General Learning Corporation, Northbrook, Illinois

Copyright © 1995 International Resourcing Services, Inc.
60 Revere Drive, Suite 725
Northbrook, IL 60062

All Rights Reserved

No part of this book may be reproduced, transmitted, or stored in any form
or by any means, electronic or mechanical, without prior written permission
from the publisher.

Library of Congress Catalog Card Number: 95-76140

ISBN 0-9646179-0-0

CREDITS

Contributing Editor: Susan K. Jones

Senior Editor: Carol Spielman Lezak

Art Director: Jill Sherman

Illustrator: Rosemary Fox

Editorial Consultant: Carole Rubenstein

Printed in Hong Kong

Contents

ear Friends,

I welcome you to Liberty Falls...and to Clara's Bakery! My little cookbook will introduce you to the best of the recipes that have made my Bakery a landmark in our Rocky Mountain mining town. And you'll share in the history, life, and lore of Liberty Falls. Believe you me, as one of the village's "Founding Mothers," I've made the acquaintance — and the good friendship — of so many of our residents. And everyone is part of the patchwork quilt that is Liberty Falls.

Now don't worry about whether you'll be able to handle the recipes I'm revealing here: They've all been tested time and time again — both for ease in baking and as crowd-pleasing favorites. After all, I surely wouldn't make anything that my favorite Bakery customers wouldn't buy!

I think you'll be pleased to find that most of these recipes need just a small number of simple ingredients — things you probably already have on your pantry shelves. I like to rely on fresh, seasonal fruits, nuts, and other flavorful items to enhance my baked goods — so no matter what time of year it is, I know you'll find just the right recipe for festive occasions or everyday treats.

I do hope you'll try these, my very favorite recipes. Every one of them has special meaning for me and the folks here in Liberty Falls. Enjoy our stories, too. By the time you finish leafing through this cookbook, I'll wager you'll feel like an honorary citizen of Liberty Falls, Colorado!

With fond regards,

Clara Goodfriend

Best Baked
Breads

very summer here in Liberty Falls there's a wonderful Baking Contest with lots of categories: pies, cakes, fruit desserts, and even one for specialty breads. I don't know quite what got into me a few years ago when the Baking Contest rolled around, and I blush to tell you this story! You see, I'd always wondered which of the many recipes I have for Irish Soda Bread was the very best of all. So I picked out five recipes from my various cookbooks and sources, and made up a batch of each one. Some had a little more flour than others, some featured raisins or other fruits, and one even used whole-wheat flour instead of white! Like I say, I was feeling a bit mischievous, so I entered all five loaves in the Baking Contest! "The best one will probably win a prize, and the others will just be also-rans," I told myself.

Well, to my surprise and eventual embarrassment, all but one of the breads took a prize: 1st, 2nd, 3rd, and 4th! When the other ladies learned what I had done, some of them were very peeved at me. I had quite a few ruffled feathers to smooth over, and finally I simply withdrew from the contest. "As a professional baker, I shouldn't really be in the running for a Blue Ribbon," I told the judges. They accepted my withdrawal, and another lady's pumpernickel was selected for first prize. But I had my triumph, after all! I finally knew — from an unbiased source — which was the very best recipe of all. Now I call it my Blue-Ribbon Irish Soda Bread.

Blue-Ribbon Irish Soda Bread

3½ cups of flour
1¾ teaspoons of salt
1 tablespoon of sugar
2 teaspoons of baking soda
2 tablespoons of butter
1¾ cups of buttermilk

It's a prize-winner, and it couldn't be simpler to make (it's even easier to eat!). Begin by mixing the first four ingredients. Then take hold of a pastry blender or fork and blend in the butter to the flour mixture. Now you're ready to pour in the buttermilk. Stir it in good, until the flour is damp. Rub some flour on your hands and lift the dough out of the bowl. Make it into a round shape because you're going to bake it in a greased round pan, 8 inches across. Place the dough in the pan, and then cut a big X across the top of the dough with a sharp knife. Bake the bread in a 400 degree oven for about 35 minutes. The top should have a nice brown color when you take it out to cool. Now, don't cut it or serve it until it's all cooled off. Your family will love to eat this sliced thin topped with creamy butter.

ur fair town of Liberty Falls has seen many a traveler and settler from the East, and one of the most beloved is none other than Mrs. Jason DuBois. A former Bostonian born in Germany, Gretchen DuBois came to this country when she was only a mite of a child. Her parents raised her good and proper in the ways of a real lady, and they all settled into Boston successfully, thanks to her papa's fine talents as a baker. I truly would like to have known Gretchen's father. His apple strudel is the very best I've ever tasted! In fact, when Gretchen brought over three strudels to the surprise housewarming party for the Reverend Watkins and his family, I'll wager the "oohs" and "aahs" were heard for miles around! She was very generous to share that strudel recipe with me.

Not long after that, I asked Mrs. DuBois if she had any special bread recipes she might be willing to part with. My, but Mrs. DuBois seemed flattered. "Why, Clara, surely *you* don't need any help from *me*!" she cried. "Yes, I do!" I replied. My bakery shelves had seen nothing but rye bread, wheat bread, oat bread, and a few other of the same old varieties for a long, long while. And rather than look for new recipes in just any old cookbook, I'd much prefer the "tried and true family heirloom" of a friend. Boston Brown Bread à la Gretchen is what she named this recipe, and I assure you that it truly is among *my* treasured recipes today.

Boston Brown Bread à la Gretchen

4 cups of whole-wheat flour
2 cups of white flour
4 cups of buttermilk
2 teaspoons of baking soda
⅔ cup of dark molasses
2½ cups of raisins
1 teaspoon of salt

You'll need four bread tins, size 3" x 7". If you want, you can cut this recipe right down the middle for only 2 loaves. Start off by mixing your flours together. Then gradually pour in the buttermilk and stir it together so it's mixed real well. In another bowl, add the baking soda to the molasses and stir that together. Next, add the molasses mixture to the first bowl. Stir it, and, finally, mix in the raisins and the salt. Put the same amount of batter in each tin and bake them in a 350 degree oven for about 35 to 45 minutes. Now, I don't sell this as day-old bread; but the truth is, it tastes much better the day *after* it's baked than the same day!

I will never forget the night Mrs. Willie Griffin — better known here in Liberty Falls as Gertie — passed out her fresh-from-the-oven homemade cookies to the voters during her husband's mayoral campaign! It's no surprise that Willie won in a landslide over his opponent, Buster Clark. Before that election day, I didn't know Gertie very well, but I was intrigued by a lady who could bake cookies good enough to influence the electoral process! One Sunday afternoon I invited her to my cottage for tea. As we relaxed by the fire in my matching rocking chairs, Gertie asked me for a special favor. "Clara, my arthritis has been acting up, and I can't bake as much as I'd like to these days. If I give you my secret family recipe for Sally Lunn Bread, will you bake me two dozen loaves for the next supper meeting of the Town Council? Keep in mind that you must keep the recipe a secret."

I enjoyed Gertie's company so much that I decided to accept the job. But much to her surprise, when the steaming loaves were passed around the tables, one outspoken council member made a motion: "Mayor Griffin, I move that Mrs. Griffin be asked to give her Sally Lunn recipe to Clara Goodfriend so that we all can purchase this wonderful bread at the Bakery. It's that delicious!" The vote was unanimous, and Gertie was so flattered that she agreed. Now this Sally Lunn Bread is one of my best-sellers, and I always donate 2 cents per loaf sold to the Town Council's discretionary fund as a way of saying "thanks"!

Gertie's Secret Sally Lunn Bread Recipe

2 cups of flour, sifted
3 tablespoons of sugar
3 teaspoons of baking powder
½ teaspoon of salt
2 eggs
½ cup of milk
½ cup of melted shortening

   This recipe is so fast, you'll be able to whip up your own Sally Lunn bread in two shakes of a lamb's tail. In a big bowl, mix together the first four ingredients. Next, separate the eggs. Put the egg whites aside until later. In a smaller bowl, beat the yolks; then pour the milk into the yolks and mix it around a bit more. Pour that into the dry ingredients, and blend it just a tad — only enough to get the whole mixture moist. Add in the melted shortening. Next beat the egg whites until they are stiff and fold them into your batter. Use a square baking pan for this bread, oh, I guess an 8" x 8" pan will do best. Bake it for 30 minutes at 350 degrees and serve it hot. This just may become *your* secret recipe!

"Waste not, want not" was one of my mother's most oft-repeated phrases when I was growing up. So I knew what I had to do one wintry day when I came across one lonely cup of rolled oats while cleaning my supply shelves. "What recipe takes just one cup of oats?" I asked myself. I couldn't think of a thing — but all that did for me was raise the question to a challenge! "I'll just have to invent something," I told myself. "That's what Mama would have done!" I'd already started a batch of my best wheat bread, so I decided to set apart one loaf's worth of dough and add some of the oats. "This bread will be extra wholesome, and the oats will add taste as well as nutrition!" I told myself, warming to the task.

Well, instead of shaping this loaf to go in the traditional oblong pan, I made it round to fit in a cake tin — and I popped it into the oven with a smile as I said to myself, "Here goes nothing!" It did turn out to be *something*, though — I saved the round loaf for our own dinner table, and Scotty and I ate three slices apiece! "This discovery is just too good to keep from my customers," I told Scotty, and he agreed. The next day I made a big batch of what I now call my Hearty Wheat and Oat Bread. And what do you know: My frugal notion turned out to be an inspiration! This delicious bread is now a true Liberty Falls favorite! Serve it with stews and other stick-to-your-ribs fare. I'll wager your family will enjoy it, too.

14

Hearty Wheat and Oat Bread

2 cups of flour
1 cup of whole-wheat flour
½ cup of rolled oats
¼ cup of sugar
3 teaspoons of baking powder
⅔ teaspoon of salt
1½ cups of milk
3 tablespoons of oil
1 egg
1½ tablespoons of rolled oats (for topping)

Now I always make sure I have enough rolled oats on hand for this bread. First, set your oven temperature to 350 degrees. Mix together the first six ingredients. Set that bowl aside and, in a smaller bowl, beat together the milk, oil, and egg. Pour that mixture into the flour mixture and stir it all around just until the dry ingredients are dampened. Spread the dough in a round cake tin 8 inches across that is greased on the bottom only. Before you pop it in the oven, top the dough with the 1½ tablespoons of oats. Bake it for about 45 minutes. The top will be golden brown and a toothpick should come out clean. Let the bread cool a few minutes before you take it out of the pan. Serve it warm.

hen business in the Bakery is slow and a customer happens by, there's nothing that brightens my day like a nice bit of conversation. One spring morning a gentleman stopped in and tipped his hat. He smiled and seemed to hesitate some. I soon learned that he spoke very little English — he was a French boarder at Mrs. Applegate's sent to learn American mining techniques for his employers on the other side of the Atlantic Ocean. After our first little talk, Jacques Rhodes stopped in frequently. One day I asked Jacques to tell me a bit more about his homeland. It seems he was born and raised in the French wine country. As you know, we don't have many exotic wines here in Liberty Falls, so I asked Jacques if he was missing the French vintages.

"Oh, Madame Goodfrand," Jacques exclaimed in his charming accent. "It eez not zee wines I mees zo much as zee — how you zay? — grapes and raisins!" Right then and there I knew I could ease Jacques' homesickness with my very best recipe for Raisin Bread. Something about this combination of ingredients accents the raisins' plump, juicy taste. I made up a batch and surprised Jacques with a slice of raisin bread and fresh butter the next time he stopped in. *"Magnifique!"* Jacques proclaimed. *"Merci beaucoup*, my dear, dear Madame Goodfrand!" Oh, the warm rewards of knowing how to bake just the right comfort foods for friends.

Homesick Raisin Bread

1 cup of water
1 cup of raisins (golden raisins taste best in this bread)
1 cup of sugar
1 egg
⅛ cup of butter
1 teaspoon of baking soda
2 cups of sifted flour

    Set your oven temperature to 350 degrees. Then put
the raisins and the cup of water in a small saucepan on
the stove and turn on the flame until the water boils.
Turn off the flame and let it cool. While it's cooling, mix
together the sugar, egg, and butter in a large bowl until
they are smooth and creamy-looking. Take out one more
bowl, and mix your flour and baking soda with a fork.
Now, you're ready to make your batter. Take half the
flour mixture and mix it into the sugar mixture. Then
add half the raisins and water. Blend that. Add the rest
of the flour; mix it in, and finally add the rest of the
raisins and water. Give it all a good stir. Take out a bread
pan that measures 9" x 5" x 3". Grease and flour it and
pour in the batter. This takes a bit more than an hour to
bake — maybe 65 or 75 minutes. Let it cool.
    Mmm, this is so tasty and fragrant. Put some out and
watch it disappear!

*T*hat Molly Brown! What a delightful character…someone I was privileged to meet when she stopped here in Liberty Falls on her way from Leadville to Denver. She fell in love with the architecture hereabouts — and as everyone knows, that lady adores fancy houses. You should see the one she and her husband have on one of the fashionable streets of Denver! Well, when Molly was here, she attended a Ladies' Discussion Club meeting we held at the library. As luck would have it, the sweet potato crop was in, and our talk turned to ways we could use those delicious potatoes since they were in such abundance. I didn't expect such an elegant lady to be an expert on baking, but Molly took charge. "Get out your writing implements, ladies. I'm going to give you the best sweet potato recipe on earth," she proclaimed with a flourish.

Turns out Molly used to be quite the hand on an old-fashioned cook stove before she married Mr. Brown and he "hit paydirt" down in Leadville. Times were so hard for her in her youth that she had to learn how to bake bread in old beat-up tins. Molly Brown's Best Sweet Potato Bread recipe was recited from memory and it works wonderfully well — one of the best-tasting sweet breads I ever tasted.

Molly Brown's Best Sweet Potato Bread

4 eggs
3 cups of sugar
1 cup of oil
⅔ cup of water
2 cups of cooked, mashed, cooled sweet potato
3½ cups of flour
½ teaspoon of nutmeg
1 teaspoon of cinnamon
½ cup of coarsely chopped pecans
3¼ teaspoons of salt
½ cup of raisins
2 teaspoons of baking soda

Mix together the eggs, sugar, oil, water, and the sweet potato. (Mmm-mmm, it already smells good, don't you think?) In a bigger bowl — big because you're going to get three loaves from this recipe — combine the rest of the ingredients. Then add the potato mixture to the dry ingredients and stir it all together until it's thoroughly blended. Grease and flour three loaf pans, and pour an equal amount of batter into each. Bake them for 1½ hours in a 350 degree oven. Your kitchen will smell delicious! You can't keep this bread a secret from your family. Serve it slightly warm for the best flavor.

Early one afternoon a few months back, our Liberty Falls Stationmaster John Strauss stopped by the Bakery, and we had quite a chat. "You know, Clara," Mr. Strauss commented, "these days the Union Pacific is bringing people to town from all parts of the country — even from way down South. One of the most enjoyable aspects of my job is meeting these folks and learning their ways!" That got me to thinking: I wasn't seeing many of these out-of-towners here in the Bakery as customers — so maybe I should offer and promote some of the treats they'd be homesick for? I wrote my favorite cousin Ellen, who'd moved to South Carolina some years back. "What recipes can you send me that will please a Southerner's palate?" I asked her. Well, Ellen loves to cook and bake — she sent me enough recipes to keep me busy for a month! I swear this is the best of them all.

Up North, we were never much on cornbread — but I know it's considered a Southern staple. As soon as I perfected the cornbread recipe, I placed an advertisement in the *Liberty Falls Daily News* offering my Southern Gold Cornbread. I considered it a great compliment when Retired Colonel Beauregard Symington — one of our Southern settlers — stopped in and made the very first cornbread purchase. The next day he returned and bowed grandly with hat in hand to thank me: "Ma'am, that cornbread brings back memories of my old Kentucky home," he said with twinkling eyes and a broad smile.

Southern Gold Cornbread

1 cup of flour
1 cup of cornmeal
3 tablespoons of sugar
2 teaspoons of baking powder
1 teaspoon of baking soda
1 teaspoon of salt
2 large eggs
1½ cups of buttermilk
⅓ cup of butter, melted

This cornbread is fluffy with a delicious, slightly sweet, nutty taste.

Heat up your oven to 425 degrees. In a large bowl, mix together the dry ingredients. In a separate bowl, beat the eggs. Then add in the buttermilk and the melted butter to the eggs. It makes a bit of a sizzle if the butter is still hot. Stir it together and then add this mixture to the dry ingredients. Stir it until the flour mixture is moistened. Pour it into a well-greased 9" x 9" pan.

In 25 minutes, you'll have the best cornbread you ever ate!

Each weekday morning around 9 a.m., my Steaming Hot Popovers come out of the oven all golden-brown and crispy on the outside — and you can just about set your pocket watch by the customers who line up to buy them while they're still warm! The ingredients are simple, and even a youngster can whip up a batch with no trouble — but the results are nothing short of magical! Those popovers puff right up in no time at all — and oh, what a treat when they're served with fresh butter! Most of my customers don't even wait to enjoy "the trimmings," I notice — especially the men. They'll pop at least one popover into their mouth even before they leave my shop!

I guess I make popovers every day because each time I take a pan from the oven I'm overwhelmed by warm memories of my late husband, George. Long before we ever left Rhode Island, I served my new husband his first popover with a plate of beef stew one evening. I'll never forget his look of consternation!

George assumed that the popover would be solid, like a muffin or scone. When he broke it open and found only an empty shell, he seemed exasperated. He didn't want to hurt my feelings, but it was clear he didn't understand the purpose of baking something so big and puffy that was mostly hollow inside. "Taste it, George," I urged him, pushing the butter dish his way. "Mmm-mmm!" was his immediate response. Four popovers later, I knew I had a "convert" at my supper table!

Steaming Hot Popovers

2 cups of sifted flour
1 teaspoon of salt
1½ cups of milk
½ cup of cold water
4 eggs

This recipe will make a dozen of these delicious hot treats. Your family will love them just as much as George did. First, you need to set your oven to 450 degrees. Then simply mix all the ingredients with a wire whisk — just until the batter is smooth. Make sure that the bottom of the bowl doesn't get ignored — scrape it up nicely. Generously grease up a muffin tin and pour in the batter — each section should be filled just about two-thirds of the way. Then you're ready to pop these popovers into the oven. After 35 or 40 minutes, you'll see the biggest, puffiest popovers you ever did see — crisp and brown on the outside.

Now, remember that they're hollow inside, and they hold in the steam a bit, so be careful when you open them up — before you slather on the butter.

Delicious Muffins & Prize-Winning Biscuits

I may be a Founding Mother of Liberty Falls, but whenever I think of my Mama's blueberry biscuits, well, I'm just carried away to the day long ago in Rhode Island when she first made them.

Back in Rhode Island, on a warm summer's day, we would take an armful of tin buckets and head out to the wild blueberry bushes a ways behind the Widow O'Hanrahan's house. Old Mrs. O'Hanrahan had a great big red brick house that her grandaddy built back before the great Revolution. He came from farming stock back in Ireland and got that house built on money he earned by raising the finest crops in six counties.

Well, we young folks thought the Widow O'Hanrahan was too old and confused to even notice that we were out back of her house, raiding the blueberry bushes. We thought we were being so downright sneaky that she'd never know that a few quarts of blueberries were about to be spirited away by the neighborhood children. We surely were surprised one day when we were tiptoeing away from her garden and there she stood — madder than a wet hen. The only way she'd let us go was if we promised to bring back some baked goods — chock-full of her blueberries. Why, that's where *this* recipe came from. Mama was in the middle of baking biscuits when I arrived at the door laden with blueberries — and a little blue around the mouth from eating berries on the way home!

Mama's Melt-in-Your-Mouth Blueberry Biscuits

1 cup of blueberries
2 tablespoons of sugar
2 cups of flour
1 tablespoon of baking powder
½ teaspoon of salt
3 tablespoons of sweet butter
1 cup of milk

In one bowl, stir together the blueberries and the
sugar. Put it aside for now. In another bowl, you've got to
sift together the flour, baking powder, and salt. Next, take
hold of two knives and cut the butter into that mixture.
When you're done, it'll look like a crumble topping. Now,
you can pour in the milk and mix it around real gently.
Add in the blueberries that you mixed with the sugar and
stir it all together real carefully — so you don't crush the
blueberries. Spread some butter on a baking sheet and
drop the batter onto it with a tablespoon. You can
probably get a dozen good-sized biscuits from this batch.
Bake 'em in a preheated oven — 375 degrees — for about
20 or 25 minutes. If you've got a very hungry family,
make up twice as many. Serve them hot and top them
with honey and butter.

ow, don't tell my customers in Liberty Falls, but I do have a few special recipes that I never use for my Bakery. This is one of them — my very own Apple Muffins, slightly modified from the recipe taught to me at my mother's knee, back in Rhode Island! These muffins were always on the table when someone needed comfort back home. And now my own son Scotty loves them just as well — especially since they're "for family only." When Scott would come home dejected after a hard day at school, or had skinned his knee playing kickball with the other boys, I'd have him sit down by the fire and wait while I mixed up a batch of these heartwarming treats.

I always put by some apples so they'll last until the harsh winter weather hits. I keep them stored in my little cold cellar — but if I run out, my friend Mrs. Applegate usually has a dozen or so she'll share with me.

You haven't truly felt winter until you've experienced the winds whipping through downtown Liberty Falls in January and February. Chaps my lips and cheeks just thinking about it! On those bitter days it's difficult to leave my warm bed at 4 a.m. to get started with my baking chores. But by the time I have the first batches of cakes, pies, and rolls in the oven, I'm good and warm — and the smiles on the faces of my customers as they burst through the door of my cozy shop make it all worthwhile, believe you me!

Warm-You-Up Apple Muffins

¼ cup of butter
1 egg
2 cups of flour
½ cup of sugar
2½ teaspoons of baking powder
1 teaspoon of cinnamon
½ teaspoon of salt
1¼ cups of milk
1 large apple, cored and coarsely chopped

Before you start mixing ingredients, there are a few small things to take care of. First, set the oven temperature to 400 degrees. Next, melt the butter in a little saucepan and then set it aside to cool. Beat the egg in a cup and set that aside also. Grease up the muffin tins (you're going to get a dozen muffins from this recipe). Now you are ready to really get going! Take all your dry ingredients and sift them together in a large bowl. In a smaller bowl, pour in the butter and egg you've set aside (mind, you must make sure the butter is cooled) along with the milk and apple. Stir it up and then pour it all into the dry ingredients. Blend it only until it's just mixed together, and you're ready to fill the muffin tin. Fill each greased muffin cup about two-thirds full and pop it in the oven. These delectable muffins will be ready to take out of the oven in only 20 minutes; the apple aroma will fill the air and their tops will be browned. You'll need to cool them in the tin for another 5 minutes before serving. Slather on the fresh butter — that's Scotty's favorite way to eat these.

Once I got started baking cornbread to please the "transplanted Southerners" in these parts, I decided that corn muffins would be another good Bakery offering. But, of course, to make a corn muffin you've got to have cornmeal. Normally that's no problem — I order up several barrels a month, and Mr. Tully down at the General Store lets me know when one arrives in his store. Then I have my hired man bring the barrel to my storeroom. That's the *usual* way things work, but one time I almost lost my last barrel of cornmeal to a crafty baker from Hickory Corners!

It seems this baker had a huge order for cornbread — a big church supper or some such event — and he wasn't as good at planning as I am. He drove his horse and buggy over here to Liberty Falls and offered Mr. Tully twice the usual price for the barrel of cornmeal that was supposed to tide *me* over until the next railroad shipment! Well, lucky for me, the Tullys value me as a customer — so they checked with me first before taking advantage of the "windfall." When I got wind of what was happening, I threw off my apron and rushed on over to Tully's just in time. The other baker was trying to load the cornmeal onto his buggy! "Don't you dare sell that meal to this out-of-town scalawag!" I scolded, and Mr. Tully sheepishly ordered the stranger to "unhand" my cornmeal! When you taste these luscious muffins, you'll understand why I refuse to do without cornmeal for even one day in *my* Bakery.

Everyday Cornmeal Muffins

⮔

1 cup of yellow cornmeal
¾ cup of flour
2½ tablespoons of sugar
2¼ teaspoons of baking powder
¼ teaspoon of salt
¼ cup of butter
1 cup of milk
1 egg white

If my customers knew how easy these are to make, why, I'm sure Clara's Bakery would never get another customer for cornmeal muffins. For a dozen medium-sized muffins, you start out by mixing together the first five ingredients — all the dry ingredients — in a large bowl. Then mix the butter into that dry mix with a fork — break up any lumps that may form. In a small bowl, mix the milk and the egg white; then pour that into the big bowl and blend it all together with your fork. Pour the batter into greased muffin tins — oh, I think two-thirds full should do it. Pop them into a hot oven — 450 degrees — for 12 or 15 minutes. They'll have a beautiful golden, lightly browned look to them when they're ready. Eat 'em while they're hot.

I'm sure you've heard Mrs. Evelyn Johnson of the Wooden Nickel Inn carrying on about that notorious Lothario, Mr. Walter Craig. Handsome and rich, that bachelor is. So all the eligible young ladies in these parts just about go crazy trying to attract his attention whenever he arrives in town on business. Most of them content themselves with sashaying around in their silk dresses and plumed hats, but one girl decided to test the truth of that old saying, "The way to a man's heart is through his stomach." Of course, she herself couldn't boil water. So she came to me and asked me to bake up a special batch of Buttermilk Biscuits. Brought me the recipe herself. Said it was handed down from mother to daughter for generations in her Southern Alabama family.

Well, the recipe looked wonderful, so I consented. Baked up the biscuits, light and fluffy as can be. (You'll see what I mean if you try them.) The young lady stopped by with her own basket and linens, and I could see she had a crock of fresh butter and a shiny silver knife in there, too. She packed the still-warm biscuits in the basket and headed on over to the Wooden Nickel Inn, where Mr. Craig was staying. Later, when I asked Mrs. Johnson what happened, she told me that Mr. Craig was polite enough to eat two biscuits, and pronounced them excellent! But the next day, he headed right out of town, exactly according to plan. The young lady was left to pine away for him in Liberty Falls!

BUTTER

Fall-in-Love Buttermilk Biscuits

2 cups of flour
2 teaspoons of baking powder
¼ teaspoon of baking soda
1 teaspoon of salt
3 tablespoons of butter
1½ cups of buttermilk

Get out your rolling pin for this recipe. You'll get some of the most delicious buttermilk biscuits you ever tasted.

First, mix together the dry ingredients. Then cut in the butter with a fork or pastry blender. Now you're ready to pour in the buttermilk. Stir it well. Dust your surface with some flour, and roll out the dough until it's about ½-inch thick. I like to use Mother Goodfriend's 2½-inch biscuit cutter that I brought with me when George and I left Rhode Island. So take your biscuit cutter and make yourself about 9 or 10 biscuits. Pack 'em in in a greased baking pan, about 10 inches square (their sides should be touching). Bake them until they are a golden brown color, about 10 or 15 minutes, at 425 degrees. You'll like these with butter and jam.

We've had some mighty famous visitors here in Liberty Falls over the years: Enrico Caruso the opera singer, Molly Brown, and even Buffalo Bill himself! Scotty was just about wild to see Buffalo Bill in the flesh, but I was afraid that the show Mr. Cody put on at the Opera House might be a bit too rowdy for such a young child as my Scott. Lucky for Scotty, he had the chance to see the Great Man right up close, for one day Buffalo Bill himself, clad in buckskins and a huge cowboy hat, stepped inside my little Bakery! "Ma'am," he said, touching the brim of his hat in a gesture of respect, "I understand you bake the best Cheddar Cheese Biscuits west of the Mississippi. I'd like a baker's dozen if you have some ready." Hearing a deep male voice, Scotty came running out from the back room and gasped, "Buffalo Bill!" The old Scout knelt down to say hello and chatted ever so gently with Scott while I put his biscuits in a sack.

"Stay here and let's talk some more," Scotty pleaded as Mr. Cody thanked me, paid for his purchases, and prepared to go. "All right, young'un, but you'll have to help me eat these biscuits!" Bill replied. What a sight! For the next hour, Buffalo Bill and my little son sat chatting right there in my Bakery and chomping cheese biscuits, one after the other. Before Bill returned to his hotel room, all 13 biscuits were devoured, and Scotty had a friend for life. Life surely is unpredictable out here in the Wild West. But these tasty biscuits are guaranteed to please. Take it from Buffalo Bill!

He-Man Cheddar Cheese Biscuits

1 cup of flour
1 teaspoon of baking powder
¹⁄₁₆ teaspoon of salt
¼ cup of butter
½ cup of cheddar cheese, coarsely shredded
⅓ cup of milk

    You'll need a really hot oven for this. Preheat it to
450 degrees. Mix together the first three ingredients, and
then cut in the butter. Your dough will look like a bowl of
crumbs. Next, add in the cheese and milk, and stir it up
until you've got a soft ball of dough. Dust your cutting
surface with some flour, and gently knead the dough on it
about 5 or 6 times. Then, use a rolling pin to smooth out
the dough to a thickness of ½ inch. Take a 2- or 3-inch
biscuit cutter and cut yourself about a baker's dozen of
biscuits. Put them on a greased baking sheet with about
1 inch of space between 'em. Poke the top of each biscuit
with a fork a few times. Bake them until the tops are
golden brown — about 12 or 15 minutes. Serve them
right away. 'Course, if you're expecting Buffalo Bill,
maybe you had better make two batches.

henever I bake these rich-tasting Pumpkin Biscuits, I bask in a warm glow of memories about my old friend Mrs. O'Brien. It was she who treated me like a daughter all those years ago when my late husband George and I first arrived in Colorado — and she let me help earn my keep by baking for her and her other boarders at her home in Golden. Mrs. O'Brien was always so kind to compliment me on my recipes and the taste of my baked goods — but she was also quite a cook and baker herself, and on those long, cold nights we'd often trade recipes as we sat by the fire and worked on our mending. Both of us were what's called "scratch" cooks — we don't really need to write recipes down because we can tell how much of which ingredients to add just "by feel." So one late fall evening, Mrs. O'Brien suggested this recipe to me. "Clara, I see we have quite a few pumpkins still left, and they'll go to waste if we don't use them up soon. Why not try some pumpkin biscuits tomorrow? I think the boarders will really take to them!" Next morning I did as she suggested, and the results were outstanding! All the boarders raved over them, so of course I shared the praise with my mentor. Now every fall, as soon as the pumpkins are ready to come in off the vine, I make up a big batch of Mrs. O'Brien's Favorite Pumpkin Biscuits and remember my wonderful friend — the kindest lady in Golden, Colorado, and the dearest friend I've ever had.

Mrs. O'Brien's Favorite Pumpkin Biscuits

1 cup of flour
1½ tablespoons of sugar
2 teaspoons of baking powder
¼ teaspoon of salt
¼ teaspoon of cinnamon
¼ cup of fresh butter
¼ cup of chopped pecans
¼ cup of light cream
⅓ cup of fresh, cooked, mashed-up pumpkin

Mrs. O'Brien, bless her heart, would always plan these biscuits as a special treat. Put the first five ingredients in a big bowl and stir them up. Then take a fork or pastry cutter and cut in the butter until it looks all crumbly. Add the nuts and stir it all again. In another bowl, mix together the pumpkin and the cream. Take a whiff; that pumpkin sure smells good, doesn't it? Add the pumpkin mix to the big bowl and stir it enough to moisten the dough. Dust your cutting board with some flour, and knead the dough very gently — just a few times will do the trick. Grab your rolling pin and flatten out the dough to about a half-inch thick and cut 2-inch biscuits. Grease a baking sheet and lay them out. You should leave space between the biscuits. Bake them until they're golden brown — about 15 to 20 minutes in a 400 degree oven. Simply grand!

At one time, Snake Eye Jake had a big crush on Lillian, the songbird of our Liberty Falls Opera House. Usually, he could hardly tear himself away from one of his all-night poker games down at the Gold Nugget Saloon. But whenever Lillian came to perform, why there was Jake — backstage for all her rehearsals — and hanging around the stage door after every performance!

Anyway, one day while Lillian was visiting Liberty Falls, Jake came into my shop. "Mrs. Goodfriend, I'm lookin' fer somethin' special," he said, averting his eyes and holding his hat in his hands. "You got any of them English things — you know, they kinda look like biscuits, but they ain't?" I knew right away Jake meant my English Scones. I had just sold my last dozen, which seemed to do Jake right in. "I'll pay you double if you c'n bake me up another dozen right quick — and pack 'em up real pretty like," Jake offered. My baking was done for the day, but I said I would — regular price. "Come back in an hour," I told him. When he came back, I didn't recognize Jake! My, he really shined himself up! Hair slicked back. A

clean shirt. No dust on his boots. And a bunch of fresh flowers in his arms. He collected his scones and headed on over to the Opera House. It's clear this was all for Lillian, because when I went to hear her sing that night, she had the flowers in a vase on the stage and she dedicated a song to her "secret admirer" who somehow knew how much she loved real English Scones!

Snake Eye Jake's Special-Order Scones

2 cups of flour	¼ cup of cold creamery
1¾ teaspoons of sugar	butter, unsalted
½ teaspoon of baking soda	¾ cup of cold buttermilk
¼ teaspoon of salt	raisins or bits of semi-sweet
	chocolate (optional)

Lillian couldn't get tastier scones in England, if indeed that's where she's from. I start out making this recipe by sifting the flour, sugar, baking soda, and salt together in a big bowl. Next, I measure out the butter and work it into the flour mixture with a fork until the mixture gets a sort of grainy look to it. The buttermilk goes in next. If you like raisins or bits of semi-sweet chocolate (you can chop up a block of chocolate), you can add in about ¼ cup now and stir them in. I stir it all together until I've got a lump of dough. I sprinkle a bit of flour onto my cutting board, and I knead the dough lightly — the way I do it, and this is what I think makes my scones taste so good, is that I just fold it, turn it, fold, and turn it. Only about 5 kneads are needed (my, I do love a bit of wordplay!). Then I pat out the dough until it's about half-an-inch thick, and take out Mother Goodfriend's 2-inch biscuit cutter. I cut a dozen scones and use every last scrap. I reshape the scraps, and cut more out of that. I put the scones on a plain baking sheet (no grease on it, if you please), and bake them for 13 to 16 minutes in a 400 degree oven. They will rise and turn golden-colored. Serve them while they are warm.

ere's another recipe that I save "just for home" — my Dinner-Fresh Baking Powder Biscuits. When friends visit for dinner, I like to serve these fresh out of the oven. They do tend to get a bit hard if they sit on the bakery shelf all day, so that's why I don't offer them to customers. If you swear yourself to secrecy, I'll tell you about one of my rare mishaps in the kitchen. It had to do with these very biscuits, which I was baking one day for a dinner with Mrs. Applegate, our town's first mayor Paul Johnson, and Mr. and Mrs. John Strauss (John's the stationmaster for the Union Pacific here locally). I was just in the midst of combining ingredients when Scotty called, "Mother, Mother!" I ran to see what he needed, and, well — it was just that he wanted to show me a pretty butterfly that was flitting around on our front porch. When I went back to the kitchen, I resumed mixing — never thinking that I'd forgotten to add the baking powder!

Well, as I told you, I like to serve these biscuits fresh from the oven. My guests were already seated at the table when I slid the biscuits right from the baking sheet into the waiting basket. Mayor Johnson took the first biscuit. I could tell from his first bite that something was wrong. I took a taste and immediately realized what I had — or rather had *not* — done! Since then I've been extra careful at the Bakery and at home to make sure all my ingredients are in the bowl in just the right amounts!

Dinner-Fresh Baking Powder Biscuits

2 cups of sifted flour
1 tablespoon of baking powder
¾ teaspoon of salt
2 eggs
¾ cup of heavy cream

After my poor story of woe, I'm sure *you* won't forget the baking powder.

Take the flour, baking powder, and salt and sift them together. In another bowl, beat the eggs. Then stir the eggs and cream into the dry ingredients. Don't overdo it! The biscuit mix will be soft and lumpy and a bit sticky. Use a tablespoon to drop the biscuits onto an ungreased baking sheet. You'll probably get about 12 to 15 biscuits from one batch. Bake them for 15 minutes in a 400 degree oven. These go fast at the breakfast or supper table.

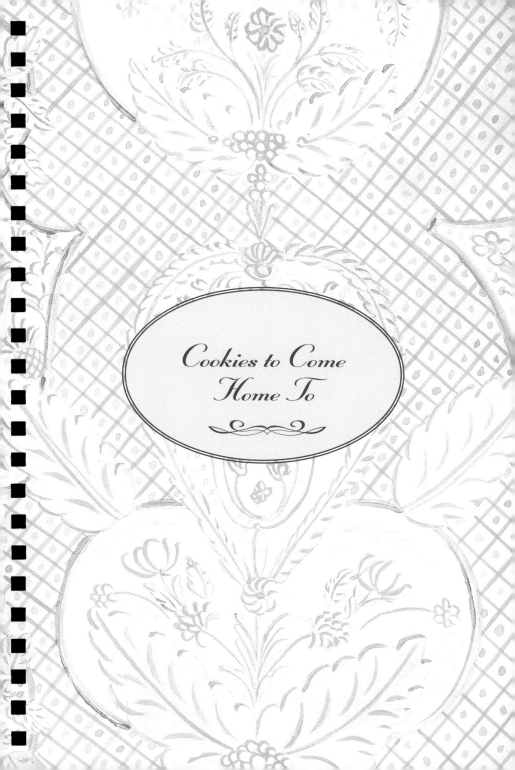

Cookies to Come
Home To

I've always held a special warm spot in my heart for Liberty Falls' most devoted schoolmarm, Abigail Martin. What other teacher would rise at the crack of dawn each winter day — almost as early as I do for my baking chores — to rush to the Clemen's School and boil up a pot of steaming hot chocolate for the youngsters to enjoy before classes? Scotty would always tell me about the extra, fun activities Miss Martin added to the regular curriculum: everything from vegetable and flower gardening to cooking! So you can imagine how flattered I was one day in February when she asked if I'd give her students a baking lesson, right here in my own Bakery workroom!

I agreed right away, and we planned for the very next Friday afternoon. The children arrived ready to roll up their sleeves, wash their hands, and start in on this simple-but-tasty recipe for Brown Sugar Cookies. Oh, it was a messy scene, what with a dozen bowls of batter being mixed all at once by novice bakers! I'll wager there was more flour and sugar on the children's aprons — and on my floor — than there was in the bowls, but no matter! While the cookies were outside chilling on the porch, Miss Martin supervised her pupils in cleaning up every last bit of their own mess! Then — about an hour later — the cookies were ready to go in the oven. Each youngster tried two or three of these tempting sweet treats while they were still warm, then wrapped up a dozen or so apiece to proudly share with their family!

Cooking Class
Brown Sugar Cookies

1 cup of light brown sugar, packed
1 cup of unsalted butter
1¼ cup of flour
½ teaspoon of vanilla
¼ teaspoon of cinnamon
a dash of salt
1 egg

Blend together the brown sugar and butter with a fork until it is smooth. Then add in all the rest of the ingredients except for the egg — save that for last. Stir the batter well. Add the egg next, and beat the mixture well. Now you have to chill the cookie dough, so put your coat on when you set the mixture to chill outdoors (you don't want to catch your death!), or store it in your ice chest for an hour or so. Don't let it freeze — just get it nice and cold. After an hour or longer, heat up the oven to 350 degrees and pull out your favorite baking sheet. Drop rounded teaspoonsful onto the ungreased baking sheet, about 12 to a sheet. These cookies really spread out while they bake, so leave room between them. They only need to bake for about 8 minutes. Then you should let them cool on the sheet for a half-a-minute before taking them off with a spatula. Do this gently and let them cool on a rack. You'll get a bit over 60 cookies from this recipe. But don't worry about waste — they don't last very long in the cookie jar!

hen I was a young girl back east in Rhode Island, Scottish oatmeal cookies were my very favorite dessert. Mother would reward me with a special batch anytime I earned a good grade or learned a new stitch at my embroidery. She had a wonderful old Scottish recipe, Mother did, and she refused to share it with anyone who wasn't kin! "This recipe is part of your heritage, Clara dear," she whispered to me when she first divulged the ingredients to me. It was just a few weeks before my marriage to George, and Mother was feeling a bit teary about letting me go. She wouldn't even write down the recipe, but made me memorize it and swear myself to secrecy. "Make these oatmeal treats often, and share the recipe with your own wee ones some day," she urged me.

If I had a nickel for every batch of Mother's oatmeal cookies I've baked over the years since then, I could retire from the Bakery, sure enough I could! And I still can't bring myself to write down the ingredients to Mother's own secret recipe — even for friends like you! I keep it just for Scotty and me — and I've used his Grandmother's own secret recipe as a reward for him, just like I remember it all those years ago. But this recipe is something special, too: It's a marvelous rendition that combines the original goodness of oatmeal cookies with two extra-special ingredients — raisins and bits of real semi-sweet chocolate that I hand-chopped from a block of chocolate. They're so good that they're always in demand at the Bakery.

46

Favorite Family Oatmeal Cookies

1 cup of butter
¾ cup of dark brown sugar
¾ cup of white sugar
2 eggs
1 teaspoon of vanilla
1 teaspoon of baking powder
1 teaspoon of hot water

1½ cups of flour
½ teaspoon of salt
2 cups of rolled oats
1 cup of bits of semi-sweet
   chocolate
1 cup of chopped walnuts
¾ cup of raisins

You can bake about 4 or 5 dozen of the tastiest cookies with my recipe. Start by heating up the oven to 375 degrees. Then put the butter and both sugars in a very large bowl and cream them well. The eggs and vanilla are added next and stirred in. In a cup, mix together the baking powder and hot water until the powder is dissolved. Pour that along with the flour and salt into the sugar mixture. Stir it all around. Finally, add in all the rest of the ingredients and stir together thoroughly. Grease your cookie sheets thoroughly and use a teaspoon to drop the dough onto the sheets. Bake these for about 10 minutes, give or take a minute or so, until the edges are browned. Let the cookies cool on the sheets for a minute before transferring them to a rack to cool. Scrumptious when they're still warm. Chewy and crisp at the same time!

ere in Liberty Falls, we know there's a special place reserved in heaven for Mrs. Stevens, wife of our own Doc Stevens. Oh, she's an elegant lady, that's for sure. Why, she was the first Liberty Falls resident ever to decorate her home with Fred Cox's fancy dining room furniture. Carved table legs, rosettes, and inlays, all the ornate trimmings! But Mrs. Stevens turned that dining room into a makeshift hospital the day of the disaster at the Gold King Mines — nursing the miners as tenderly as if they were her own sons. And on any given afternoon she's just as likely to use that beautiful table to roll bandages for the Doc as she is to be serving high tea. The lady does like to hold genteel parties for her friends, though — and I'm proud to say that I've often been invited to her handsome, blue-roofed home.

The little cottage I share with Scotty is much too small for me to reciprocate with the same kind of grand entertaining, so I thank Mrs. Stevens for her hospitality by baking "a little something" each time she invites me to tea. One of her personal favorites are these Raspberry Cocoa Tidbits — which make the perfect "sweet bite" after finger sandwiches, scones, and tea. The first time I brought them to Mrs. Stevens' home, all the ladies raved over them so enthusiastically that I decided they'd be a fine addition to my Bakery offerings. Even the miners who live at Mrs. Applegate's have been known to relish these tiny tidbits — although they tend to polish them off a dozen or so at a sitting!

48

Raspberry Cocoa Tidbits

⅔ cup of sugar
8 tablespoons of butter
2 teaspoons of vanilla
2 eggs
1 cup of flour
½ cup of unsweetened cocoa
½ teaspoon of salt
raspberry preserves

I'll bet that Mrs. Stevens would be surprised at how simple the ingredients are for this delicious tea-party cookie.

Start by setting your oven temperature to 350 degrees. Then beat together the sugar and butter until it's smooth. Next, add the vanilla and eggs. You'll need to use your arm muscles again to beat these ingredients until they're well-blended. (I like to use a whisk.) Add in the rest of your ingredients and this time stir with a spoon or fork. Make sure that they are blended until the batter is smooth. Grease up the baking sheets and drop rounded teaspoonsful of the batter onto the sheets. These cookies spread out a bit, so be sure you leave space, maybe 2 inches, between the cookies. Put some flour on the back of a spoon and flatten out the cookies a bit before baking them. Then spoon about a half-teaspoon of raspberry preserves on each cookie. My Cocoa Tidbits bake up fast — it only takes about 6 to 8 minutes to bake up a batch. Cool them for a minute on the sheets, then take them off and cool them on a rack. This recipe makes about 3 dozen cookies.

My experience with dentists is that they're always warning their patients to stay away from sweets — why, you'd think they themselves lived on nothing but apples, carrots, meat, and potatoes to hear them tell about it! I don't mind telling you, it gets me a little worried as a professional baker. After all, where would Scotty and I be if everyone in Liberty Falls gave up cookies, cakes, pies, and other sweets? But I happen to know for a fact that our resident tooth doctor hereabouts — George Barker, D.D.S. — has a secret sweet tooth. Why, it was George himself who gave me this recipe for these Sweet-Tooth Cookies! In fact, the sweeter they can be made, the better he likes 'em. That's why I added chocolate bits to my version of his mama's recipe.

Dr. Barker told me that his mother perfected this recipe when he was a young boy — and he enjoyed them with a glass of milk several times a week after school when he was a lad. It's always heartwarming to me to discover what foods bring special comfort to my friends — and in most cases, it's the sweet baked goods that really bring back memories of the old home fires, security, and ease. These cookies are a breeze to make, and the ingredients are probably already in your pantry — so why not try them soon?

Sweet-Tooth Cookies

3 cups of flour
1 teaspoon of baking
  powder
¼ teaspoon of baking
  soda
½ pound of butter
2 tablespoons of oil
1 cup of sugar

3 eggs, beaten
1 teaspoon of vanilla
2 teaspoons of lemon
  flavoring or extract
1 cup of chopped walnuts
⅔ cup of bits of semi-sweet
  chocolate
sugar and cinnamon

In a large bowl, stir together the first three ingredients. In another large bowl, cream together the butter and oil, and add in the sugar. Stir that well. Now, add in the eggs, vanilla, and lemon flavoring. Stir again. You're ready to add the flour mixture to the liquid ingredients. Stir it together, and mind you don't let some of the flour land on the floor! Finally, in go the nuts and the chocolate. After you've mixed the dough, divide it in half. Cover it and let it chill several hours or overnight. When you're ready to bake, set your oven to 350 degrees, and get out two long cookie sheets. Take each piece of dough and form it into a long rectangle about 4 inches across and an inch high. Sprinkle them with sugar and cinnamon and bake them (each on a separate cookie sheet) for 20 or 25 minutes. Take them out of the oven, slice them into pieces about ¾-inch wide, turn the pieces on their sides, and bake them for about 5 or 10 minutes longer.

ost Liberty Falls folks think of Tom Slaughter, the foreman of the Gold King Mines, as a rough-and-tumble gent. But whenever I spy Tom with a gingerbread man in his hand, he looks just like a little boy! You see, every Saturday noon, Tom and the other miners get their paychecks. (You know what they say about the Gold King: "Never a payless Saturday!") On his way home, Tom stops in here at the Bakery to reward himself with a special weekend treat: a bagful of my fresh-baked gingerbread men! One afternoon, while Tom was chomping on his first spicy cookie, he told me about how his ma used to make the same wonderful treat when he was a boy back in Eureka, California.

I had a notion to ask Tom if he'd ever tasted the moist, cake-like gingerbread that's baked in a pan and served in squares. "No, ma'am, but it sure does sound tasty," Tom replied. "When you come in next week, I'll have some ready for you," I promised Tom — then I spent the following days experimenting to come up with the perfect pan-baked gingerbread. That Saturday, Tom showed up like clockwork. He was so impressed with my gingerbread that he almost forgot to order the two loaves of wheat bread he'd come in to purchase. "Dee-licious, Mrs. Goodfriend!" he pronounced. "The taste is almost like Ma's gingerbread!" Tom told all his Gold King friends about my gingerbread, and now it's become one of my tried-and-true items — especially on Saturdays!

Almost-Like-Ma's Gingerbread Squares

1 cup of dark molasses
1 cup of sugar
2 tablespoons of shortening
2 eggs
1 teaspoon of cinnamon
1 teaspoon of ginger
1 teaspoon of cloves
3 cups of flour
2 teaspoons of baking soda
a dash of salt
1 cup of boiling water

No cookie cutters needed for this recipe ... just a big baking pan. Set your oven to 350 degrees, and grease and flour a large baking pan, about 13" x 9". It's easiest if you use a fork to cream together the first three ingredients in a large bowl. In a smaller bowl, beat the eggs. Then add them and the spices to the sugar mixture. Next, in go the flour, soda, and salt. Mix that around real good. Finally, pour in the boiling water and stir it in well. When the oven reaches the right temperature, you're ready to bake. Pour in the batter and bake it for about a half-hour or 35 minutes. I like to serve these gingerbread squares warm with fresh whipped cream, or with a pint of the finest vanilla ice cream from Greller's Pharmacy.

While I treasure the peace and quiet here in Liberty Falls, I must admit that we do have a few colorful characters who keep things interesting. Indeed, our newspaper editor Oliver Cummings once told me, "If it weren't for Snake Eye Jake and that sly cattle rustler Jimmy Olson, I'd be hard pressed to write much of anything exciting except meeting notices and obituaries!" I've already told you about how Snake Eye Jake "went soft" and nursed a crush on that fancy opera singer, Miss Lillian. Well, I also have a tale to share about Jimmy Olson — in fact, this recipe for Apricot Bars is what brought that rascal Jimmy to my mind!

It was Mrs. Tully — the lady who runs Tully's General Store with her husband — who gave me this superb bar cookie recipe. Oh, these cookies are so mouth-watering with their sweet apricot flavor. All the while she was talking me through the ingredients, Mrs. Tully was gossiping to beat the band. "I hear tell that nasty Jimmy Olson's going to take himself a bride. Land sakes, can you beat that?" the lady told me in a stage whisper. "The girl's from back east, and it appears to me that she has no idea at all what Jimmy does for a living. Poor thing's in for a mighty big shock!"

Well, Jimmy and his bride left town right after the wedding — I think he was afraid folks hereabouts would let on to his new missus what he was really like. So we don't see much of him in town these days, but I can't stir up the ingredients for this recipe without old Jimmy Olson popping into my mind!

54

Cattle-Rustler's Apricot Bars

1 cup of oatmeal
1 cup of sifted flour
⅔ cup of packed brown sugar
½ teaspoon of baking soda
½ cup of butter, melted
½ cup of apricot preserves

There aren't many baked goods that make a kitchen smell as sweet as these apricot bars. Get started by heating up your oven to 350 degrees. Then mix together the first four ingredients in a large bowl. Next, stir in the melted butter. Press about two-thirds of this crumbly mixture into a baking pan that measures about 8" x 8". Now, get out a tablespoon and drop the preserves all over the dough. Spread it around, almost up to the edges of the pan. Then crumble the rest of the dough over the preserves and press it down gently. Pop it in the oven and bake it for a bit more than a half an hour — about 35 minutes is usually how long I bake it. After it cools, cut it into squares and serve it with a steaming-hot mug of coffee or tea...mmm, mmm!

ave you ever seen a rhubarb plant?
They *are* exotic looking with their big, curly leaves —
almost like what I'd imagine growing in a jungle. When
left to themselves they can become quite large. I've never
laid eyes on one as big as the rhubarb plant in Caroline
Smithers' backyard, though — why, it's nearly as tall as
Scotty was at the age of 6! Caroline is the niece of my
dear friend Mrs. Applegate, and we all were over at her
home one evening rocking on the porch when the
subject of rhubarb came up. "I've heard that rhubarb is
good to eat, Clara, but I confess I simply don't know what
to do with it. Should I stew it, boil it, serve it as a
vegetable, or is it more of a dessert?" Caroline asked in
confusion. I'll admit I was stumped at first, too — but
that night I lit my lamp and searched through cookbook
after cookbook, looking for an answer for Caroline.

"Eureka!" I shouted when I came across a recipe for
Rhubarb Oatmeal Cookie Bars. The next day I asked
Caroline to cut a few rhubarb stalks from her plant
(without the leaves — those should be left out in the
garden), and I took some rhubarb to try the cookies. With a
few adjustments — I can't resist making adjustments to
recipes! — I came up with the ideal combination of
ingredients. I rushed a batch over to Caroline, who savored
every bite of her first rhubarb oatmeal treat. In thanks,

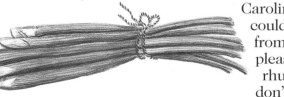

Caroline promised me I
could help myself to rhubarb
from her plant anytime I
pleased! If you have a
rhubarb plant in your yard,
don't let it go to waste.

Rhubarb Caroline Cookies

1 cup of flour, sifted
1 cup of brown sugar
¾ cup of rolled oats
1 teaspoon of cinnamon
½ cup of melted butter
1 cup of water
1 cup of white sugar
3 tablespoons of cornstarch
1 teaspoon of vanilla
3¾ cups of rhubarb, cut up into small pieces

Have an 8" x 8" baking pan ready and heat up your oven to 350 degrees. In a bowl, mix together the first five ingredients. Take half of this mixture and press it down into the baking pan. Put that aside, and get out a saucepan; put in the water, white sugar, cornstarch, and vanilla. Cook it up over medium heat until it's nice and thick. While it's cooking, spread the little pieces of rhubarb over the dough. Then pour the thickened sugar mixture over the rhubarb. And on top of that, crumble the rest of the cookie dough. Ready to bake? You sure are. Bake it for about one hour. You can eat this warm or cold — my customers like it both ways. Caroline likes it best topped with a scoop of ice cream.

I've been in the Bakery business so long now that just about every recipe I make has some sort of memory or story attached to it. When it comes to my Walnut Fingers, it's my assistant Jenny who has the tale to tell. Or maybe that should be *tail* — since the story involves a passel of hungry Liberty Falls squirrels! As you know, when I first opened the Bakery, I couldn't afford any help. I baked everything myself and then waited on customers all day long in the store. But once I'd established a regular clientele, I was able to hire a few young ladies — always women who could especially use the job. It's my way of doing a good turn just as my "adopted mothers," Mrs. O'Brien and Mrs. Applegate, once did for me.

Jenny was one of these new employees, and in just a few days' time she proved herself an excellent baker. Good with customers, too — for she had a sparkling smile and a kindly manner. But one day, Jenny decided to set out a tray of freshly baked Walnut Fingers to finish cooling on the Bakery's back porch. She turned around for just a minute to take another batch out of the oven and — in the wink of an eye — those Liberty Falls squirrels made off with every cookie! Jenny was afraid I'd never forgive her, but I just laughed. "All I ask is that you learn your lesson, Jenny girl! Those squirrels have good taste!" I told her. Now I invite *you* to try the Liberty Falls squirrels' favorite cookie recipe. And I assure you, humans love them, too!

Nut-Lovers' Walnut Fingers

1 cup of flour
1 teaspoon of baking powder
¼ teaspoon of salt
¼ cup of butter
1 cup of light brown sugar, packed
1 egg
1 teaspoon of maple flavoring
⅓ cup of chopped walnuts

Get ready by greasing and flouring an 8" x 8" baking pan. Oh, yes, don't forget to set your oven temperature to 350 degrees. In a medium-size bowl, sift together the first three ingredients and then set it aside. In a large bowl, first cream the bit of butter, then add in the brown sugar and cream these two together. Beat the egg in a cup and then add it and the maple flavoring to the butter/sugar mixture. Now you can add in the flour mixture. Be sure to put some muscle into this to mix it well. Finally, the most important ingredient — the walnut pieces. Stir them in. Spoon the dough into the baking pan and press it down with your fingers. I know, this does get a bit messy, but if you put a few drops of water on your fingertips, you'll have an easier time of it. Bake for about 25 or 30 minutes; then you'll be ready to cool it in the pan for 20 minutes. Flip it out of the pan and slice it into 16 "fingers" to finish cooling on a rack. And the last step: Keep it away from any squirrels!

Cakes, Crisps,
& Cobblers

ack when I first opened Clara's Bakery, I felt it was important to advertise, especially in the *Liberty Falls Daily News*. I struck a deal with the editor and publisher, Oliver Cummings, and I'd write my own advertisements to appear twice weekly. Sometimes I'd just write about a baked-goods special or sale price — but every once in awhile I'd "dream up" something to create excitement. One time I promised a dozen free cookies with every 10th apple pie purchased on a certain Friday. Another week I offered folks a jar of my homemade preserves if they'd buy any three loaves of bread. But the idea that attracted the most attention of all was when I set up a baking contest.

Business had been pretty good for several months — so I offered the enormous prize of $10 for the very best item entered in the contest. Since by then I knew just about everybody in town, I promised to judge the entries "blind" — in other words, I'd have no idea who baked what. Well, as it turned out there were nearly 50 entries! I tasted them all once and then narrowed the field down to five of the finest treats of all. Then I tasted those five again, and ranked them for the $10 Grand Prize as well as four runners-up. When the winner was announced, a red-faced Oliver Cummings stepped forward. "Sorry, Clara, I couldn't resist entering my Aunt Emma's Apple Crisp — it's an old family favorite from back in Ohio." Being the editor of the newspaper, Oliver didn't feel right keeping the prize money, so he donated the money to the Clemen's School.

Daily News Apple Crisp

2⅓ pounds of cooking apples, peeled, cored,
    cut in quarters
1 cup of sugar
1 tablespoon of lemon juice
¾ teaspoon of cinnamon
⅛ teaspoon of ground cloves
1 heaping cup of flour
⅛ teaspoon of salt
¼ pound of butter
¾ cup of walnut pieces

    Aunt Emma's recipe is a special favorite from the bakery. I've followed her recipe exactly. First set your oven to 375 degrees. And while you're waiting for it to heat up, grease a rectangular 2-quart metal baking dish with some butter. Cut up the apple quarters into slices and mix them in a large bowl with the cloves, cinnamon, lemon juice, and only ¼ of the cup of sugar (save the rest of the sugar for the next step!). After you've mixed it all together, pour the apple slices into the baking dish. In another bowl, you'll be mixing the topping. Stir together the flour (the flour should equal one cup and 2 tablespoons), salt, and the rest of the sugar. Use a pastry cutter and mix in the butter. The topping will look crumbly. Now you can add in the walnuts. Spread your topping over the apples and then pop it in the oven. It will take about 45 or 50 minutes, maybe a little more, to bake. Check the crust to make sure it's browned and crisp on top. It's well worth the wait. Serve it warm. If you want to, pour a little heavy cream on it.

id you ever hear tell of a more colorful town name than Blackberry? Well, I never did either until Mrs. Edna Barclay moved to Liberty Falls with her husband, the new accountant for the Gold King Mines. Edna was such a kindly sort, and such a good "spinner of tales," that she soon joined my little circle of friends for chats and tea parties. One afternoon Edna started reminiscing about her childhood days back East in the tiny town of Blackberry. It came as no surprise to me that they put on a Blackberry Festival there every year when those plump, juicy, dark blue-purple berries were ripe! Before she got finished describing all the blackberry pies, preserves, cakes, and cobblers, all our mouths were watering! "Just you wait, ladies — when I get my hands on some blackberries this summer, you're in for a wonderful treat," Edna laughed. "I'll bake you up a batch of the recipe that won me the Young Lady's Blackberry Prize when I was just a slip of a girl of 17!"

Edna was as good as her word...and one warm and breezy August afternoon several of us ladies gathered around Edna's old oak dining table to sample the promised Blackberry Cobbler. The "oohs" and "aahs" kept up until the pan was empty, and then Edna kindly gave each of us the recipe written in her elegant handwriting. I haven't changed so much as a pinch of any ingredient she specified — I consider this dish the closest thing to "blackberry heaven" there is!

Blackberry Festival Cobbler

1 quart fresh blackberries	1 teaspoon of baking
1 cup plus 2 tablespoons	powder
of sugar	⅛ cup of sugar
3 tablespoons of cornstarch	¼ teaspoon of salt
1 tablespoon of butter	⅛ cup of butter
¾ cup of sifted flour	¼ cup of milk

Bring back that taste of real home-town baking with this recipe!

Start by heating up your oven to 400 degrees. Take out your favorite 2-quart casserole dish and pour in those fresh berries (don't forget to wash 'em first and pick out any stems). In a bowl, mix together the cup and 2 tablespoons of sugar and the cornstarch; then put that mixture into the casserole and stir it with the berries. Place dots of the butter on the berries and let it stand for about 20 minutes. In another bowl, sift the rest of your dry ingredients together. Cut in the last amount of butter on the ingredient list with two knives or a fork, and then stir in the milk until the dough becomes stiff. Give the blackberries a good stir (to mix in the butter that dots the top). Then start putting the dough over the berries by dropping tablespoonsful over the top evenly. Pop this treat into the oven for 30 minutes. When it's ready, the top will be a light golden brown and the berries will be bubbling away. Cool it off well before you put it out on the table. Better have plenty of vanilla ice cream to serve with this. You can get 4 to 6 servings from this recipe.

You've probably already read about the wedding of Suzette DuBois and Fred Clark, Jr. — why, it was the society event of the decade here in Liberty Falls! Just imagine: the daughter and son of "Clark and DuBois" themselves — our bigwig bankers in town — falling in love and getting married! Both Mrs. Clark and Mrs. DuBois enjoy putting on airs now that their husbands are so successful, but I don't hold it against them. I've seen those old sod cottages outside of town which both ladies lived and worked in while their husbands started the bank in the rough-and-ready early times hereabouts. These days, they've got upstairs maids, downstairs maids, cooks, and seamstresses — but back then, they did for themselves and theirs.

Anyway, back to the DuBois-Clark wedding. Mrs. DuBois honored me with the opportunity to bake the wedding cake, and I was very anxious to please. "Suzette insists on a carrot cake, of all things, Clara," Mrs. DuBois reported with a worried shake of her head. Well, I've had experience with the odd special request by a nervous bride, so I visited the DuBois mansion and had a baker-to-bride chat with Suzette. I convinced her that traditional white cake was best. And I told her I'd bake my special carrot cake, to take with her and her groom on their wedding trip.

Both Suzette and Fred loved my Carrot Cake — they each sought me out after the honeymoon to tell me so — and I'll wager you will, too!

Honeymoon Carrot Cake

1 cup of shortening
½ cup of brown sugar
1 egg, beaten
1 tablespoon of water
2 cups of grated carrots (2 good-sized carrots)
½ teaspoon of baking soda
½ teaspoon of cinnamon
½ teaspoon of nutmeg
½ teaspoon of salt
1½ cups of flour
1 teaspoon of baking powder

Of course, you don't have to be a newlywed to enjoy this cake. It's a favorite here in the Bakery. Here's how you make it. Cream the shortening and add in the brown sugar, egg, and water. Next, mix in the grated carrots, baking soda, cinnamon, nutmeg, and salt. Add the flour and baking powder, and mix well. Pour the batter into a greased loaf pan or a small mold and chill it overnight. (If you chill it out on your porch, you'll want to make sure the temperature doesn't drop to freezing!) Heat up your oven to 350 degrees and bake it for one hour. You'll know it's done when you stick in a toothpick or a clean straw to check and it comes out clean. Let the cake cool before removing it from the pan.

efore our first town mayor, Paul Johnson, arrived in Liberty Falls, Albert Buck was the one and only lawyer anywhere around. And while Albert was quite a hand at creating deeds, obtaining patents, and settling mining disputes, he really shone in the courtroom. Very eloquent, and never at a loss for words: That's our Mr. Buck. Whatever the topic under discussion, Albert Buck has something to add. And that even extends to recipes! One minute he'd be telling me about a memory from his youth, and the next minute he'd say, "Take down this recipe, Clara — I think you'll enjoy baking it!" Well, the first recipe of Albert's I tried was also the last! He hinted that he'd keep his secret family recipe for Pound Cake just between us, but I happened to find out he'd also given it to Mrs. Applegate, several ladies from the First Congregational Church, and even that pesky baker who once tried to take my barrel of cornmeal right off the porch of Tully's General Store. Guess he's so proud of that pound cake, he wants us all to try it!

No offense to Albert, but this Pound Cake recipe is even better than his. You see, once I learned that everybody

and his brother had Albert's recipe, I decided to come up with an even richer, more delicious version to sell in the Bakery. It's all in the balance of ingredients I use. Now, if you share this recipe with your friends, that's all right. (I haven't really patented it.) But I'll understand if you keep it to yourself — it's special enough to become *your* old family recipe!

Clara's Patented Pound Cake

1 pound of powdered sugar
1 pound of butter, softened
6 eggs, room temperature
3 cups of sifted flour
1 teaspoon of vanilla

I'll bet even Albert likes my pound cake better than his family recipe, it's that rich. Have a 10-inch tube pan ready and get the fire going in the oven to heat it to 350 degrees. The rest is so easy that on the days I plan to offer this in the bakery I usually have time to make up another special item for the bakery shelves. First, I cream the sugar and butter until they are smooth. Next, I add the eggs, and beat the mixture well. Now it's time to add the flour. Gradually add in the sifted flour, stir it well, then pour in the vanilla, and blend that in. You don't need to grease the tube pan, so just pour in the batter. Cut through it with a knife to keep air bubbles from forming inside the cake. Then bake it for an hour and a quarter. Use a wooden toothpick to test if it's done. (Better buy your toothpicks from Tully's General Store. His deluxe toothpicks don't have any splinters!) Don't remove it from the pan until it's cooled off. In the summer, this is delicious served with fresh berries or sliced peaches.

ack East, one of the most wonderful times of year for cooks and bakers is that short season when fresh peaches are at their peak! The fruit tastes like velvet on the tongue, and that peach fragrance is sweet as perfume. Mother and I used to bake "peach everything" while the fruit stayed ripe — and then we'd can some of the remainder and put up some of the rest as preserves. I know they call Georgia "the Peach State," and I've met folks from down there who go into rhapsodies of delight describing the fruit they've grown, picked, and eaten around about Atlanta. But I've never heard anyone rave about a Colorado peach, have you?

Now, I'm not one to complain about what's available fresh here in Liberty Falls; this is a wonderful growing climate for many fruits and vegetables. Yet there's something about those peaches from back home or from down Georgia way...so when a bushel or two of fresh peaches arrives for me via the Union Pacific, I jump into a frenzy of "peach baking"! Of all the peach recipes I've tried over the years, I recommend this one most highly — it's a real peach of a dessert, if you don't mind my little pun. There's nothing quite so luscious as this cake created with peaches ripe off the tree. I assure you my customers agree. All I need to do is put up a sign outside the Bakery declaring "Fresh Peach Cake" or "Fresh Peach Tarts," and the traffic in and out of here increases in a matter of minutes!

A Peach of a Tart

1 cup of flour
¼ pound of butter
2 tablespoons of milk
2 tablespoons of sugar
½ teaspoon of vanilla
¼ teaspoon of baking powder
2 pounds of fresh ripe peaches, skinned
¼ cup of sugar
2 teaspoons of flour
1 teaspoon of cinnamon

No cookbook is complete without a recipe for a tart. So, get out a 9-inch tart pan (a pie pan will also do). First, heat your oven to 350 degrees. In a large bowl, mix together the first 6 ingredients. Chill the dough for a few hours if you can before the next step, which is to press it firmly in the pie pan. Now you can work with the peaches. Cut the peaches in quarters and arrange them over the dough. Mix the last three ingredients together and sprinkle the mixture over the peaches. Place a few dots of butter over the top and off it goes into the oven for 45 to 60 minutes.

Now, don't forget to save the peach pits in case you want to try your hand at raising a peach tree.

ver at the Logans' Land Surveyors and Assay Office here on Main Street, Liberty Falls, they're really quite a high-falutin' bunch! Especially compared to their early days when they did their work from a little tent they'd pitch out amongst the gold discovery points! They've built that elegant building of theirs, with its polished wood floors and brass spittoons; why, the place is so fancy now that they had to hang a sign outside proclaiming, "Miners Welcome." Otherwise those unshaven, dirty miners were almost afraid to step inside and check their claims or discoveries! To help "warm up their reputation," the Land Surveyors and Assay Office has taken to serving the miners refreshments and fresh, hot coffee. And I'm all for it — especially since it means a weekly order for the miners' favorite baked goods: apple pies, gingerbread cookies, and this Spicy Raisin Cake!

You know, it gives me a special thrill to be able to provide our miners with some home-baked desserts. As you may remember, the whole reason I came to Colorado in the first place was to be with my late husband, George, while he tried to "strike it rich." I truly believe George might have been one of the lucky ones with a big claim — if his life hadn't been cut short by the Civil War. A Confederate bullet put an end to our dreams one long-ago day, but I still have a warm spot in my heart for the miners. They remind me so much of my dear George! They say my Spicy Raisin Cake really hits the spot after a hard day's work! See if you agree with them.

Strike-It-Rich Spicy Raisin Cake

1 cup of warm water
1 cup of sugar
1 cup of raisins
¼ cup of butter
1 teaspoon of cinnamon
¼ teaspoon of ground cloves
½ teaspoon of salt
2 cups of flour
1 teaspoon of baking soda
1 teaspoon of baking powder

The taste of this cake is like pure gold, according to the prospectors who frequent the Land Surveyors and Assay Office — and it's easier to make it than it is to pan for gold. Turn on the oven to reach 350 degrees. Put the first seven ingredients in a saucepan and bring them to a boil. Let the mixture boil for 1 minute and then turn off the flame, and take it away from the stove to let it cool. When the liquid is cool, sift the other ingredients together in a bowl and then mix the liquid with the dry ingredients. Grease a 9" x 9" cake pan and pour in your batter. It bakes up in only an hour. This cake has a real nice simple flavor, and it's just the thing to go with a mug of fresh-ground coffee from Tully's. And if you want to fancy it up for dinner, put on your favorite butter cream frosting.

Not only is Doc Stevens one of the best "sawbones" in three states, but he's a mighty nice person, too. I'll never forget the "prescription" he ordered for James Killoran, that new homesteader with a parcel of land west of town. When Doc stopped in my bakery one day, he said, "Clara, I think you've met Mr. Killoran?" I nodded yes — I'd seen this sad-looking man in church with hat in hand, a tear rolling down his cheek from time to time as he sang from the hymnal. "Well, he came to me feeling poorly, but I can't find anything wrong with him. Except his heart. Killoran's heart is fixing to break because he misses his wife Bertha and their children.

"The sooner he gets that homestead cleared and the house built, the sooner his family can join him. But we've got to get him back on his feet, and I think you can help, Clara. Could you fix James your very best Strawberry Shortcake and get Scotty to deliver it to him, nice and fresh? I think that will do the trick; Mr. Killoran's been reminiscing to me about the strawberry patch out back of his home and how wonderful Bertha's shortcake is. Send me the bill, Clara — and let me know what happens!" Well, as usual, Doc was right. Scotty and I both went out to the homestead to deliver the shortcake, and Mr. Killoran looked at us with such warm thanks, I felt the tears welling up in my eyes. That was several years ago — and today the Killorans are all Liberty Falls residents with one of the nicest homesteads you've ever seen! Now, why don't *you* try Doc's "prescription"?

Strawberries-and-Cream Shortcake

❧

1½ cups of flour
⅓ cup of sugar
½ cup of cold unsalted butter
1 egg
strawberries, blueberries, or any summer berry
whipped cream

First, heat your oven to 350 degrees. Then, mix together the flour and sugar. Cut up the butter into tiny pieces and then cut the butter into the flour mixture with two knives. Next, stir in the egg. Dust your rolling surface with some more flour, and knead the dough gently until the dough is smooth. Now you are ready to take a rolling pin to the dough. Roll it out to about ¼-inch thick. These shortcakes are usually about the size of a nice saucer from your good set of china, so you'll need a cutter that's about 4 or 5 inches across. You'll probably get about 6 shortcakes out of this recipe. After you cut them, lay them out on ungreased baking sheets and bake them for only about 15 minutes. Be sure to place them in the center of the oven. When they're done, the undersides will be a lovely golden brown. Cool the shortcakes on a rack and when you're ready to serve them, heap on the berries and cream. I felt so for poor James, I copied down this recipe and gave it to him to send home to Bertha, who I'm sure missed him just as much as he missed her.

I never spent much time studying literature and poetry as a girl. I'd been raised up much too practical for that. It wasn't until recently that I discovered the charms of a well-turned phrase, thanks to our elegant Liberty Falls visitor, Herr Friedrich von Buren of Germany. Herr von Buren is a celebrated poet. He was touring American towns to lecture and do readings from his leather-bound volumes. In Liberty Falls, he stayed at the Wooden Nickel Inn and did nightly readings for the churches, ladies' societies, and even one or two of the gentlemen's lodges. Between you and me, I wasn't planning on going to hear him read — couldn't see the sense of it. That was until Herr von Buren stopped in here at the Bakery.

With his top hat and courtly manners, he cut quite a figure in my doorway. As luck would have it, I had just baked several Streusel Cakes for his reading that night at the library. As Herr von Buren made his selections, I told him he'd also be tasting one of my European specialties that very evening! The next day the gentleman appeared at my door with an ear-to-ear smile. "*Frau* Goodfriend, your Streusel Cake transported me back to Munich! *Danke, danke!*" He handed me a piece of parchment. "Here is just a small token of thanks." The poet had written me my very own verse about sweet baked goods from a lady named Clara! I blushed with pride — and made up my mind to attend every one of his readings from then on! Now I invite you to try the cake that inspired the first and only poem about Clara Goodfriend!

Special Occasion Streusel Cake

1 cup of sugar
¼ pound of butter
2 eggs
2 cups of sifted flour
2 rounded teaspoons of baking powder
½ teaspoon of salt
¾ cup of milk
4 tablespoons of flour
4 tablespoons of sugar
⅛ pound of butter

I can still hear Herr von Buren groaning with pleasure at the taste of this cake! I was very proud that evening! Well, I'd better get on with telling you how to make this cake. Set your oven to 350 degrees and grease and flour a baking pan that measures 13" x 9". Cream together the cup of sugar and the quarter-pound of butter. Then add one egg and beat well. Add the other egg and beat again. In another bowl, you can sift together the flour, baking powder, and salt. Mix that in bit by bit to the sugar/butter mixture, alternating with the milk. When you've got it all mixed together, pour it into the pan. The rest of the ingredients make the streusel topping. Just mix 'em up in a small bowl, and then sprinkle it over the top of the cake. Bake for one hour and when you're done, you'll be groaning, too — maybe from eating too much of this delicious cake!

Blue – Ribbon
Pies

I never would have believed that anybody had to be taught to make a Basic Pie Crust. Why, it's been like second nature to me since I was old enough to wield a rolling pin! Mother taught me to mix dough "by feel" — a handful of this, a pinch of that — so when I first got the letter from the Whitman White Flour Company, I didn't know what I'd do! Seems this famous flour company in Topeka, Kansas, had gotten wind of my "baking prowess" — that's what they called it — from one of their salesmen who passed through Liberty Falls. They offered me $150 — imagine! — just for the privilege of printing my "secret" pie crust recipe on their white flour bags. Well, as you can imagine, I was floored. The sum was enough to take my breath away. It would mean real financial security for Scotty and me! But then the reality set in. I'd have to write down my recipe and be sure all the quantities were right, so anybody could make a good pie crust without fear of failure.

It took me a few tries, I'll admit. I got self-conscious trying to measure out the cups and the teaspoons instead of working by handfuls and dollops. But the results were good: I'll stake my reputation on it! The Whitman White Flour Company has been printing my recipe for years now with nary a complaint and lots of thank-you letters. My favorites are from young brides who amaze their new husbands with "pie crust just like Mother used to make." Try it. I know you'll find the results delicious.

BEST FLOUR xxxx

My Secret Double Pie Crust

2 cups of flour
1 teaspoon of salt
⅔ cup of shortening or butter
¼ cup of cold water

In a large bowl, mix flour and salt with a fork. When that's done, cut in ⅓ cup of shortening with two knives or a pastry cutter until the shortening and flour form small balls the size of large peas; then cut in the remaining shortening. Dribble cold water into mixture while stirring with a fork. Keep on stirring it until all the dough is moistened and sticking together. Divide it equally to form 2 large balls.

Next, you'll need 2 sheets of pastry cloth each about 16 inches square. Flour each sheet lightly. Roll the first ball out between the 2 sheets so that it is large enough to extend at least ½-inch beyond edge of an 8- or 9-inch pie plate. (Roll from the center outward.) You may have to dust the dough with flour to prevent sticking. When the dough is completely rolled out to about ⅛-inch thick, pull off top cloth. To get the crust into the pie pan, slide your hand under the cloth, invert the pie pan over the crust, hold it together, and flip the pan over. Now, roll out the top crust as above. Add the filling to your pie. Moisten the edges of the bottom crust with a bit of water. Carefully fold the top crust in half, and then in half again. Place it on the pie with the point in the center, and unfold it. Pinch the crusts together, trim the extra pieces, and, with a sharp knife, make several cuts in the top of the pie before baking.

I thank the Lord every night that Scott and I had the good fortune to find our way here to Liberty Falls after my "adopted mother" Mrs. O'Brien died. I'll never forget the day I received the letter and railway tickets from dear Mrs. Applegate inviting us to come to this wonderful town. Now Thanksgiving is a special time for me to recall these special blessings — so like the Good Book says, I take extra time then to "Do Unto Others." I've made it a tradition to bake up as many pumpkin pies as my Bakery shelves will hold. Then Scott and I bring the pies to the homes of Liberty Falls folks who are in need: be they sick, old, poor, or just lonely.

I used to make squash pies, but my pumpkin pie is a new treat that actually is very old in origin! Recently our town's first mayor, Paul Johnson, was cleaning out some ancient trunks that his Aunt Isabella shipped out to Liberty Falls on the Union Pacific. Seems Paul's Great-Aunt Agatha from Massachusetts had passed on and bequeathed the contents of the trunks to her favorite great-nephew, Paul. The contents were homely: old letters, maps, diaries, and other personal sundries. But in one of the diaries, Paul found a brittle, old, folded-up piece of foolscap with a recipe for a pie. Correspondence showed that the recipe dated from the 1600s — 'way back to the Plymouth colony. Paul asked me to try it, and after some time spent deciphering the handwriting, this splendid pie was the result. Now it's my Thanksgiving staple! You'll like it, too!

Plymouth Rock Pumpkin Pie

Bottom pie crust for a 9-inch pie pan
2 cups of cooked, mashed pumpkin, cooled
⅔ cup of sugar
1 teaspoon of cinnamon
⅛ teaspoon of ground cloves
2 eggs
1⅓ cups of whole milk

I assure you that your fine efforts in making this pie will be repaid with the looks of pleasure on the faces of those to whom you serve this delicious dessert. Prepare your pie crust and place it in the pie tin. And while you're at it, set your oven temperature to 400 degrees. Then, in a large bowl, mix together the next four ingredients. Break the eggs and add them to the bowl, and stir them in well. Add the milk and blend it all together. Pour the pie filling into the pie shell, and you're now ready to bake it. After it's been in the oven for about 15 minutes at 400 degrees, turn down the temperature to 350 degrees and then bake it for about another hour, until the center of the pie puffs up. Be careful not to burn it. Let it cool completely before serving it. Then watch it disappear!

As a professional baker, I feel I must make it clear that I've never quite seen the point of a pie-eating contest. Surely nobody really *tastes* a pie that he's gulping down as fast as possible, and all *I* can think about is the poor baker who invested her loving care just to see some big eater devour her masterpiece in 10 seconds flat! That said, I'll also admit that I *did* provide a goodly number of pies recently for the fund-raising fair benefiting the Opera House. After all, I didn't want to seem like a "wet blanket," and lots of the ladies in town were donating pies baked in their own kitchen. Favored to win the contest was Clarence Rollinside — and if you could take one look at Clarence, I think you'd understand why. Well over six feet tall with a barrel chest and a monumental belly, Mr. Rollinside is renowned in Liberty Falls as a big eater: I'll never forget watching him down two dozen chicken legs at last year's Fourth of July picnic!

Anyway, against my better judgment, I stayed around to watch the contest after dropping off my contribution. Oh, things got messy! And if the truth be known, part of that was *my* doing. It was raspberry season, and I baked a whole slew of my wonderful Raspberry Pies. Can you just imagine? Deep-red raspberries all over the contestants' faces and hands and clothing! I'll admit the contest turned out to be lots of fun — but I'm glad I wasn't poor Mrs. Rollinside, who had to wash her husband's raspberry-stained shirt after he took home the first-place prize!

Opera House Raspberry Pie

Your favorite pie crusts, top and bottom,
    for a 9-inch pie pan
4 cups of fresh raspberries
¾ cup of sugar
2 tablespoons of flour
2 teaspoons of lemon juice
⅛ teaspoon of nutmeg
2 egg yolks, beaten

    I still have to stifle a giggle at the thought of poor
Mr. Rollinside just covered from head to toe with my
delicious raspberry pie. It was rather a waste of perfectly
good raspberries, but it was for a good cause. And
Clarence has since become a steady customer for my
pies. You can't ask for an easier pie to prepare. Set the
oven temperature to 400 degrees. Get your pie crusts
ready, mix together the raspberries, sugar, flour, lemon
juice, and nutmeg. Fill the pie, and put on the top crust.
Cut a few slashes with a sharp kitchen knife and lightly
brush the top of the pie with the egg yolks. Bake it until it
is nicely browned — about 35 to 45 minutes at 400
degrees. Serve it with some ice cream or whipped cream.

*I*t's hard to believe that my "little" Scotty now stands six feet tall and graduated last spring from the Clemen's School! Why, it seems like only yesterday I was rocking him on my knee — but now he's just about grown and ready to seek his fortune! On Scott's graduation day, I invited all our friends, special teachers like Abigail Martin, and all Scotty's classmates for an outdoor party at our cottage.

Planning the party food was easy enough, but what would I serve for dessert? As the "renowned" baker in these parts, I knew my son and his guests would be expecting something memorable — and special! It should definitely be something the graduate loves, I thought. Considering Scotty's most beloved treats, I narrowed my choices down to two. "He's always been partial to apple pie, and whenever I make a batch of pecan cookies they disappear in a flash," I said to myself. "Why don't I invent a new recipe that combines both apples and pecan cookies?"

The result was this Apple Pecan Cookie Pie — and when you bake it I swear you'll agree it tastes just like a regular apple pie with a great big pecan cookie on top! If you and your family enjoy these flavorful treats, I'll wager your face will light up just like Scott's did when he bit into his graduation treat. And it looks like this pie is fixing to become a Liberty Falls tradition: Already several mothers have asked if I would bake these delicious cookie pies for their own offspring's graduation day next spring!

Apple Pecan Cookie Pie

4 cups of apples, peeled and sliced
2 tablespoons of brown sugar
1 teaspoon of cinnamon
1 cup of flour
¾ cup of sugar
½ cup of butter, softened
1 egg
⅓ cup of chopped pecans

Here's a pie that's easy as pie to make. That's why I like it as much as Scotty does! Heat up your oven to 350 degrees and grease an 8-inch pie pan. Put the apples in the pan. Mix together the brown sugar and cinnamon in a cup and then sprinkle it over the apples. Next, stir together all the rest of the ingredients. The dough will look like cookie dough. Divide it into 4 pieces and place them over the apples. With your fingers, gently press down the dough so it covers all the apples; then join all the edges. Bake this for one hour and then let it cool. Ice cream or heavy cream makes this an extra special dessert.

*I*f you've ever strolled down Main Street in Liberty Falls, I'll bet you were impressed by the architecture of the Land Surveyors and Assay Office. Mother Logan remembers very well the days when she and her family did business from a muddy old tent, and she made sure that when they had the money, the family business would be housed to befit her elegant taste. That lady is a real creative dynamo — and her ideas extend even to her baking! I'm going to share one of Mother Logan's own inventions with you here. But first, let me tell you how I got the recipe in the first place!

One early autumn afternoon, I dropped by the Land Surveyors and Assay Office to deliver the baked goods the Logans regularly order for their customers. I got to chatting with Mother Logan, and I allowed as how those poor tomatoes in my backyard would never get a chance to ripen in the cold fall weather. "Here's the perfect recipe for you, Clara," Mrs. L. volunteered — and before I knew it she'd scribbled down these instructions for her Autumn Green Tomato Pie. Why, it was so scrumptious I made dozens of these pies to sell in the Bakery — and every last tomato found good use! In fact, the pie's gotten so popular in these parts I now plant a dozen tomato plants yearly to meet the demand.

I owe a lot to my good friend and customer Mother Logan!

Autumn Green Tomato Pie

Your favorite pie crust
  for top and bottom
2½ cups of coarsely grated
  green tomatoes
1⅔ cups of brown sugar
½ cup of golden raisins
5 tablespoons of lemon juice

3 tablespoons of flour
¼ rounded teaspoon of
  ground ginger
¼ teaspoon of allspice
¼ teaspoon of salt
grated lemon rind,
  1 lemon's worth

    This pie may have a lot of ingredients, but it's a truly simple pie to make. Before you start on making your pie crust, you must drain all the juices you can from the tomatoes. Plan on doing this the day before (or at least 5 hours before) you want to make this pie. Put the grated tomatoes in a strainer or a colander and let them sit all night to drain. Next day, prepare your favorite pie crust — or try my recipe that's in this book. You'll be baking this in an 8-inch pie plate, and you'll need a top and a bottom crust. Put the bottom crust into the pie plate. Heat up your oven to 450 degrees. Now you're ready to mix up the filling; this is the easy part! Just stir together the tomatoes with all the rest of the ingredients, pour it all into the pie plate, and cover it with the top pie crust and flute the edges. Take a fork and prick some holes in the top crust and you're ready to bake. Start by baking the pie at 450 degrees for 10 minutes. Then turn down the heat to 350 degrees and keep baking it for 40 more minutes. I guarantee you'll never save *all* your green tomatoes for just pickling again!

hen I visit the Clarks in their lovely Victorian-style home, I can hardly believe that this same stylish couple once lived in a dugout "soddy" — stayed there for years until the Clark, DuBois Bank & Mint was firmly established in Liberty Falls. Sometimes over tea, Samantha Clark will reminisce about those days. No, she doesn't miss the snakes or other varmints, nor the dampness of the old place — but there *was* something romantic and adventurous about conquering the Old West in the early days of our fair town. Back then, cooking and baking had to be simple. After all — the chores around the house were almost never done, and Samantha already had several youngsters to care for. One of the special treats Samantha would make for the family back then was her Buttermilk Pie — and she still bakes it regularly to please her husband. Even though she has a cook now, Samantha won't trust making *this* pie — Fred's favorite — to anyone but herself.

When I first enjoyed this creamy pie, I wanted the recipe — but I didn't dare ask for it. Some foods are just too special, "for family only," and I didn't want to impose on Samantha that way. But I just couldn't get her Buttermilk Pie out of my mind. It's so simple, yet it has a very unique and satisfying taste. Samantha must have read my mind because one day when she was in the Bakery and I mentioned — for the hundredth time, I guess — how much I liked it, she asked, "Clara, would you like to have the recipe?" My customers couldn't be happier!

Just-for-Fred Buttermilk Pie

Bottom crust for a 9-inch pie plate
1½ cups of sugar
¼ pound of butter
¼ cup of flour
3 eggs
⅔ cup of buttermilk
2 teaspoons of vanilla

Samantha's children always call this Papa's Pie, as if it were the only pie Samantha ever made for Fred. Around the Bakery, though, we always call it Just-for-Fred Buttermilk Pie. In fact, once Fred came into the shop and bought two of the pies — just to see if I'd changed the recipe. I did not — I was faithful to Samantha's version.

Prepare your pie crust and place it in the pie plate. (Don't use too shallow a pie tin; it may overflow a bit.) Then, in a good-sized bowl, cream together the first three ingredients. Beat the eggs together in a small bowl, and add them, the buttermilk, and the vanilla to the creamed mixture and mix it all well. Pour it into your pie shell and bake it at 350 degrees until it's set. That would be about 40 to 50 minutes. (Set a cookie sheet on a rack below it in case it overflows while baking.) The top will look slightly puffed and browned. Just smell that wonderful aroma! Serve it all cooled off or chilled with whipped cream and fresh raspberries and blueberries for an extra-special treat.

've met some resourceful folks in my time, but none could compare to Boris Yadvigich — a peddler who made his living trading foods and contraptions of all kinds. He also sharpened knives from the back of his horse-drawn cart, and that's how I first happened to meet him. I was home at the cottage one day when Boris appeared at my door. "Any kitchen knives to sharpen, ma'am? I'll do a fine job of it — just 12 cents apiece!" Boris offered. Well, I let him sharpen several dull knives and invited him to stop by the Bakery and sharpen knives there, too. "Oh, you're Clara of Clara's Bakery!" Boris exclaimed, his eyes lighting up. "Listen to this — I have some wonderful pecans I got in trade for some farm equipment last week. They were fresh off the train from Georgia." I asked to try the pecans and Boris was right. They were so crunchy and richly flavorful I promised to make a trade for the whole 25-pound sack.

Next day, after he'd sharpened my Bakery knives, Boris and I struck a bargain and he left with five loaves of bread, three dozen Scottish oatcakes, and two pounds of maple fudge. Heaven knows what he traded those for, but I didn't have much time to spend wondering. I went on a "pecan baking rampage" and soon had a sign outside my Bakery door: "Fresh Pecan Pie." Those pies sold out in a matter of hours, but I'd saved enough pecans to bake one more as a thank-you for Boris — and I presented it to him, still warm from the oven, before he left town!

Peddler's Pecan Pie

Pie crust for the bottom only of a 9-inch pie plate
3 eggs
1 cup of light corn syrup
½ cup of brown sugar
1 tablespoon of melted butter
1 teaspoon of vanilla
1 cup of pecan halves

I'd wager that if Boris had my pecan pies to peddle, he'd make his fortune easily. That's a mite boastful, but folks in Liberty Falls buy them up fast every Thursday when I advertise them in the *Liberty Falls Daily News*. You can make this pie in a hurry if you need to — only the pie crust takes any time at all. Beat together the eggs slightly and then just mix them together with all the ingredients except the pecans. Pour the mixture into the unbaked pie shell. Arrange the pecan halves in a pretty pattern on the filling and, *"voila,"* as my French friend Jacques Rhodes would say, "ze pie ees raidy to bake!" Bake it for about three-quarters of an hour at 350 degrees. Best make sure you have plenty of pecans on hand, because you'll want to make this pie again and again.

"Shoofly, don't bother me, for I belong to somebody!" Every time I take out my recipe for Shoofly Pie, that old song rolls through my head. I just can't help it! Maybe you're aware that there really is such a thing as a shoofly pie — it's used to keep the flies occupied. In fact, our own Mr. Stubbs, the blacksmith, sets one out to keep those pesky creatures away from the horses while he shoes them. He puts his own shoofly pie out by the fence — and the flies stay occupied for hours! "You know, Mr. Stubbs," I told him one time, "I have a Shoofly Pie recipe that's much too tasty to leave out for the flies. Stop by the Bakery next Monday and I'll have one ready for you!"

I often do this with people in town who are not regular customers — figure out a recipe that's sure to intrigue them and then invite them into the Bakery to try it. Many times that's all it takes to win them over — and those same people will become weekly or even daily buyers! Well, that happened with Mr. Stubbs, too; one bite of my delicious pie was all it took to "make him a believer." "Why, Mrs. Goodfriend — I thought all there was to this kind of pie was pouring molasses into a tin to keep the flies away. But you're right. *This* dessert is much too good for those pesky flies! Wrap up two of them, if you please — and you can bet I'll be back for more!"

Tempting Shoofly Pie

Pie crust for the bottom of a 9-inch pie pan
1¼ cups of sifted flour
¾ cup of light brown sugar, packed
⅓ cup of butter
¼ teaspoon of salt
⅔ cup of boiling water
½ cup of molasses
½ teaspoon of baking soda

Charlie Stubbs' shoofly pie may tempt flies, but *my* shoofly pie surely tempted Charlie. Why, he even apologized for calling *his* concoction a pie at all!

After you set your oven temperature to 350 degrees, you can put your pie crust in the pie pan. But you must make sure that you make the edges high and fluted to hold the filling inside the pie. Mix together the flour, sugar, and salt, and then add the butter. Use two knives or a pastry cutter to cut the butter in. Spread ⅓ of a cup of this crumbly mixture evenly in the bottom of the pie shell. Then in another bowl, mix the water, molasses, and baking soda. Pour that over the inside of the pie shell, and finish by sprinkling the rest of the crumbly mixture over the pie filling. Move the oven rack into the very middle of your oven, and then bake the pie for 35 or 40 minutes. The top will be browned well. Let it cool. You can put this out to serve while it is still a bit warm, or you can chill it. Either way, with a scoop of Greller's Premium vanilla ice cream, it is the best you'll ever eat.

Index